Gone With the Tides

Gone With the Tides

and
Other Southern Stories

Capt. Gill Autrey

Photographs by
Lane Autrey

Lane & Company, LLC
Apalachicola, Florida

Gone With the Tides

ISBN:978-0-615-67829-0

Published by
Lane & Company, LLC
1 Scipio Creek Drive
Apalachicola, Florida 32320

Printed by
Colson Printing Company
711 North Oak St.
Valdosta, Georgia 31601

www.captgill.com
www.laneautrey.com

Dear Reader:

Some of these stories are reprinted from a newsletter I used to write for the no longer published *St. George Island Times.*

We wish to dedicate our little book to our children with love and affection, and to acknowledge our good friend, Stanley Cooper. Without his help and guidance y'all wouldn't be reading this. Our Proofreader-in-Chief, Dale Julian, proprietor of Downtown Books in Apalachicola, tirelessly corrected our many grammatical errors, for which we are truly thankful.

Capt. Gill and Lane
September, 2012

CONTENTS

Gone With the Tides 1

Home by Sunday Afternoon 3

Turpentin' St. George Island 5

Roastin' Ears 9

Mullet Heads.. 13

Gulls on the Causeway 17

The Expanse Across the Bay 21

Mama and the Retirement Home 25

Dog Years 29

Mama's Gone 33

Shopping List 37

Grammer 41

Cyber Space 45

Susan and Ramsey 49

Gorgeous George and Grandmamma's Penny 55

In Country Christmas 59

Knives 63

September 11th 69

Rock and Roll Is Here to Stay 73

The Red Belly Lounge and the Great Mullet Smoker
    of the Mouth of the Suwannee 77

Have Fun! 83

The First Last Great Armadillo Race 85

Poached Sheepshead Recipe 90

About the Autreys 93

GONE WITH THE TIDES

Margaret Mitchell's "Gone With the Wind" was, to my way of thinking, a story of the end of the agrarian society in the South. After the ~~War of Northern~~ *Civil War* ~~Aggression~~ the South joined the industrial revolution. The noted agrarian Wendell Berry in his work "The Unsettling of America: Culture and Agriculture", laments the loss of values of the agrarian life on the family farm in the South. My family was involved in turpentine and farming for several generations and I remember as a child all our food was locally grown, but through the years I witnessed the demise of a way of life and an ethos I longed for as I grew older. So a little over fourteen years ago I gave up the "Big City" and moved to Apalach.

Apalachicola's commerce waned during Reconstruction with the advent of the railroads, etc., but a viable seafood industry continued to survive and even thrive as families worked seafood houses and fished the River, Bay and the Gulf on their boats. So here still lives the spirit of independence and self-reliance that, if you will, built this Country. Families were not scattered throughout industrial centers searching for jobs to survive, and many local folks go

back with pride many generations. As other seafood ports
fell to developers, Apalach was "forgotten" as we like to say
and managed to avoid "prosperity" for the sake of the
environment and became a treasured gem scarcely to be
found these days.

I reunited with Lane, a wonderful photographer whom I
met briefly at the University of Georgia in the late 1960's,
and we started Capt. Gill's River Cruises. Aboard Lily, a
28' Adventurecraft houseboat, we share with folks the
beauty of the 246,000 acre estuarine preserve nurturing the
Apalachicola Bay.

We hope y'all enjoy these stories. See y'all on the River.

Your friend,
Capt. Gill

HOME BY SUNDAY AFTERNOON

It took me a long time but I finally realized what Alice found after her journey to "Wonderland." You know my favorite time of the week? Sunday afternoon about 5PM, because for thirty years I came to St. George Island and Sunday afternoon I would have to pack up about 5PM and drive "home". There was nothing I hated worse. Not long ago I was sitting around with some of my "foreign" friends and they were commenting, "It takes about three and a half hours to drive home, or it takes me seven, etc." Pretty soon I said it takes me about twelve minutes. They looked at me kinda daggerdly and didn't speak to me for a while.

Once I hooked up my boat and drove eight hours to a little island in South Florida for a ten day vacation. It took twelve hours to get home because I blew out a hub on the boat trailer. (If I blow out one here I leave it at the ten-foot hole and call Pendleton's Citgo and Tommy comes and fixes it.) Well, the island was beautiful and the people were really nice and the fishing was really good, when you weren't getting run over by a cigar boat or a jet ski. My friends didn't come with me and I missed them and Mama and my dogs and a lot of other things, so after three days we got the "ET's" (that's not the DT's) and I packed up, thanked everybody, forfeited seven days of rent and drove back to "Wonderland."

I have a friend on St. George Island who is one of the few real natives and I was talking to him on the phone one day and he said, "Well, I've got to go, I have to run over to the United States and get a part for my car." I though, that's it! You can go to the Most Beautiful Island in the World (not according to me but according to Conde' Nast Travel Magazine) and you don't need a passport, no jet lag, no Montezuma's revenge, no airport (the famous Southern humorist, Lewis Grizzard, never would fly. He said even the building was named 'Terminal'. Not so funny now, is it?), no security gate, no cancelled flight, no weather delays.

We always think the water is greener in the other bay, and it is. If you go over to St. Joe Bay, it is, and the scallops are delicious but it won't be long before you'll be wanting some Apalachicola Bay oysters and, alas, you will have to drive a whole twenty minutes. Business folks on the Forgotten Coast tell me they have more deals in the works than ever, so it looks to us as if folks have been to "Wonderland" and found that what they wanted all along was in their own "back bay." Or maybe they are just heeding President Bush's advice to go ahead with your business and recreational plans. Being the great patriot that I am, I think I'll get Lane and go fishing. See you on the flats.

TURPENTIN' ST. GEORGE ISLAND

There was this corn stalk plant that I've had for years, I don't even know how long, but it up and died the other day. I've got no idea what was wrong with it, but all its life it was in a clay turpentine pot that came from St. George Island.

Now everybody thinks the history of the Forgotten Coast is fishing and shrimping and oystering and they're right, but at one time the Turpentine Industry was big in this area. Most people don't know about it because it's a long gone era and most of it was so rural that a lot of folks never saw it. Believe it or not my Daddy and Granddaddy were in the Turpentine Business, and in fact Granddaddy turpentined St. George Island for Ed Ball of St. Joe Paper fame. So that clay pot was probably one of Granddaddy's. They quit using clay pots in the late 20's and went to tin cups so that tells you how old that thing is.

Now Daddy was born in 1915, and he told me that Granddaddy brought him to Apalachicola one summer when he was about 12, so that would be 1927. Anyway Granddaddy was working the Island, so he left Daddy with an old fisherman in Apalach and they went out every day in an old wooden row boat. (I doubt Mr. Evinrude had invented his outboard yet. You know how *necessity is the mother of invention*, well according to the story, Evinrude had a gal he was courting across the river and he was trying to figure a way to get over there faster than rowing so he came up with the first outboard motor. Well I bet the true story is she was married and he got caught one day. Now you can row pretty fast when you're being shot at, but not fast enough. Sometimes a load of buckshot in the posterior is the *real mother of invention*.) Pop told me you wouldn't believe the fish they caught back then. The old gentleman had a wire basket on the front of his boat and they built a fire in it at night and went flounder gigging. I wish I knew who the old gentleman was.

I'll bet it was something working trees on the Island back then during the summer. They probably had to employ non-swimmers. The way the deal worked is they would gash pine trees with a thing called a hack and attach a cup at the bottom. Gum would then ooze out into the cup. Workers would come along with a Hoover wagon loaded with barrels and pulled by a mule. They would scrape the gum out of the cups into the barrels. Now you may ask, "How in the world did they stand the mosquitoes and the sand gnats?" Well, the answer is the gum stuck to every thing so pretty soon they had a protective coating. They would then take the gum to the still, boil it, and the vapor would go up and condense through copper tubing and become turpentine. What was left in the vat was rosin (there's a similar old timey process using corn that you have probably heard about). Have you ever heard of cooking baked potatoes in rosin? Well that got started because the workers would bring potatoes to work in their overalls and throw them into the vat of boiling rosin. When they floated to the top they would be done so they would fish them and eat them for lunch.

Anyway that's a bygone era. But you will notice trees all over the island, especially in the Plantation, with Turpentine Faces.

And if you're lucky enough you may find an old clay pot with a hole in the rim, so it could be hung on a nail on a pine tree. Little St. George is a good place to look. I was down here in the bay several years ago and some mentally deficient person lit a charcoal grill on Little St. George and went off and left it. The wind blew it over and the whole Island burned. It was an unbelievable sight to watch. Folks tell me they found a lot pots after that "uncontrolled" burn.

Well that's the end of our history lesson for today. If I don't get back to my day job I'll have plenty of time to write. I don't think I'll buy another corn stalk plant to go in my pot. Instead, I think I might build a little still and get some corn and fill that old pot up with something mighty tasty.

ROASTIN' EARS

L ane and I both do a lot of cooking so here's some easy dishes we thought y'all might enjoy. Degree of difficulty - one martini = *, two martinis = **, etc.

Steamed Shrimp *

First you run down Dean because he will have some of Quentin's shrimp fresh off his boat (we say they slept in the bay). Get some large or jumbo and leave the heads on.

Put one layer of shrimp in a pot and sprinkle Old Bay Seasoning generously, put in another layer etc. Don't add any extra water.

Cover and cook over medium low heat, check every little while and stir. This takes 20-30 minutes, but you won't believe the natural juices that cook out and steam the shrimp.

Baked Fish **

This is a good one for our area. Get some fresh fish filets. Put some olive oil in a pan, put in the filets and pour some olive oil on the fish, squeeze lemon or lime juice and sprinkle them with Old Bay Seasoning, coat them with a layer of mayonnaise, and sprinkle generously with parmie john cheese. Bake in oven uncovered at 350 degrees until cheese is crusty and fish is flaky. This is a good one.

Baked Eggplant *

Slice an eggplant longwise. (I used to grow eggplant and one year I had one that had a mutated growth and the thing looked just like Richard Nixon.) Make cuts in the meat with a knife and pour in some olive oil and put face down in a dish. Bake uncovered at 350 degrees for about thirty minutes, take out and turn over with a spatula and put on some jalapeno peppers and sprinkle generously with parmie john cheese and bake for about ten more minutes.

Eggplant Casserole ***

This can be a main course. Cut an eggplant longwise. Scoop the meat out with a spoon and save the shell. Cube the meat and put in a pan with water and boil until soft and clear. Add whatever you want to. I suggest herbs from Lane's garden, spring onion, bell pepper, Roma tomatoes, celery, and mushrooms (I've had ** and I can't remember what else I put in it so just make something up.) Cook all this down, and then beat some egg whites and fold them in and put all of it back in the shell and spread goat cheese over the top and bake uncovered at 350 degrees for about 30 minutes. A lot has to do with the moon. You know how you dig a hole some times and all the dirt won't go back in the hole. That happens with this eggplant deal so just freeze the leftovers.

Roastin' Ears*

Get some corn in the shuck. (Remember the old song about the farmer that caught three thieves in his corn field; one had a bushel, one had a peck and one had a roastin' ear tied around his neck.) Put a big pot of water on a fish cooker outside and get it boiling. Cut the silk end off the ear and throw the corn in the pot with the shuck on. Get some real butter and melt it in a pan and get a table with the butter, paint brush, salt and pepper and paper towels. Fish out an ear of corn and shuck it back. All of the silk will come off. Wrap the husk with paper towels for a handle and present it to your clientele, let them brush down the roastin' ear with butter, sprinkle with salt and pepper, and let them hit it like a corn picker goin' down the row. Keep a garbage can close by. Do this in the winter with a bushel of raw Indian Pass oysters and it takes as many *'s as suits you.

Well, I had my famous secret family recipe for seafood gumbo next, but that will have to come later because Lane just got home and I have to go finish supper.

Happy eating.

MULLET HEADS

I just finished reading a book called "Mullet Heads" by Michael Swindel. It was a Christmas present. I guess its sorta like Jimmy Buffet's Parrotheads, except instead of being a celebrity groupie you're a fish groupie. Now there's the rub. Mullet is the only known fish with a gizzard, which, if cleaned properly, is a delicacy. I personally love them. In fact some Mullet fishermen down around Tampa were arrested for netting Mullet and thus violating the Net Ban, but their erudite attorney got an expert on the stand to *aver* (that means testify) that birds have gizzards, but no fish were known to have gizzards *ergo* (that's a legal term that means therefore) Mullet are not fish, they are birds. (They fly, don't they?) Case dismissed.

Now, I've told you that my newsletter is neither a religious nor a political forum so we won't debate the merits of the Net Ban biologically, but maybe you will agree that culturally it was the demise of a way of life for many a Florida Cracker. Some folks think I invented the gill net and so it was named for me. That's not true. Some folks also think I'm kin to Gene Autry. That's not true either, but some

folks think I'm kin to the south end of Champion when he's
headed North. Now that's probably true.

I never know how I get interested in things but a friend
of mine was shrimping around Alligator Point with a Bird
Dog Boat or a Mullet Boat, i.e., a boat with the motor
mounted in the bow so the back would be a table for the net
free from any obstructions. Naturally I had to have one, but
being young with a family, my yachting budget was not
particularly augmented. However, I did have an Air Boat
named "Jane Eyre," that I could use for negotiations, so I
found a homemade Bird Dog Boat at Panacea and suggested
that the Nautical Architect might swap his craft for mine. He
agreed and I pulled out with my new mullet boat with a bill
of "sail" that said in the line "price", "none, this was a traid".
I loved that boat and named her "Miss Kerniebelle" after my
daughter. We caught a lot of shrimp and mullet in it until it
met with a horrible misfortune. I came in from fishing late
one night and I parked my boat on the street, *legally*, and
went to bed. About 2 a.m. I heard a terrific boom and ran to
the window and to my dismay my Mullet Boat was gone!
Then I looked down the street and there it was on the
sidewalk. Some guy had rounded the corner and ran into the
back of my boat (it was his third DUI in a month). It was
doing pretty good until the trailer tongue hit a telephone pole
and the trailer stopped dead, but my boat didn't, it skidded
several feet further down the sidewalk. The insurance
company totaled my boat, so I had cash money burning a
hole in my pocket. I jumped in my truck and headed for
Chiefland, Florida, and Tremblay Boat and Cabinet Shop,
the builders of the Cadillac of Mullet Boats. Leo Tremblay
is a short, thin man and I never saw him in anything but a

pair of pants and suspenders, no shirt. He came from Maine where he built rowboats and all I ever got out of him is he was in Palm Beach teaching tennis lessons and wanted a place where he could "leave my shirt tail out' so he landed in Chiefland. I never understood why that was a problem since I never saw him with a shirt on. About a month later I had a brand new 24-ft. Tremblay with a shrimping pole at the net table. For the next several years I mulleted and shrimped all over Apalachicola Bay. I used to shrimp at night and it was a religious experience to be on the bay on a clear night with the sky covered with stars, and I would turn out the lights on the boat and the phosphorous coming out of the stern and into the net looked like someone was under the boat with a spot light. It was like being in God's Giant Cathedral of Nature.

Well, the Net Ban came and Tremblay Boat and Cabinet Shop went. Leo's ninety something and he lives with his son.

I never had high blood pressure until the Net Ban and I sold my Tremblay and quit mulleting and shrimping. Still the best medicine I know is to find a dock on the bay and sit there and watch the mullet jump and listen to them belly flop. No body really knows why they like to jump, but the best guess is they jump just for the hell of it. That's the only way a Mullet Head can explain his action a lot of times, "It just seemed like the thing to do at the time." Or according to Mr. Swindle, "The defining characteristic of a Mullet Head, is that they hear what the Mullet hears just before it rockets out of the water and enjoys until the belly flop."

GULLS ON THE CAUSEWAY

Well it's that time of the year again and I know I usually use this newsletter as a means of cheering you up, but I've got a problem with something I just have to talk about. BIRDS!!!!

The beautiful gulls are back on the St. George Island causeway nesting and having families. Last year we had terns and rarely seen oystercatchers, but this year it's just gulls probably because the terns and oystercatchers had enough of witnessing the murders of their Husbands, Wives, Daddies, and Mamas. We have either got blind people driving across the causeway or descendants of Adolph Hitler. If folks come down here for a relaxing vacation and can't slow down for a few short minutes and look at the beautiful birds then they need to keep their south end of a north bound horses' selves wherever they came from.

Now I must tell you, I'm no saint. I used to hunt, but I don't anymore. I really don't have any problem with people that do, I just got enough of seeing things killed. So the most serious thing I do now is catch a few fish and throw them in the "hot grease." I used to raise quail commercially for hunting plantations since you can hardly find wild birds now days.

Anyway I sent my precocious daughter to one of those elite private colleges up North and as I used to say I was paying about $25,000 a year to make her a North-East Needle-Nosed Pseudo-Intellectual (in the words of the Honorable Governor George C. Wallace). Well all those folks up there were in shock when they found out that her father sold these birds to be slaughtered. Well I told them they would have never been born if it weren't for my enterprise. I gave them the gift of life (I also gave them the gift of death). Well anyway every time I sent them a tuition check from the proceeds of bird selling, they cashed it faster than Sherman's ride through Georgia. It was sorta like the time the Kentucky Derby winner gave the whole purse to his church and the media asked the Pastor what he thought of the church getting tainted money and he said, "It taint enough." By the way, they wrote me one day and said, "Dear Mr. Autrey, We regret to inform you that it is necessary to augment your daughter's tuition." And I thought, "Thank God, I've been scared to death they were going to raise it." That's the way college folk' talk. Like the time I didn't do so well at a major Southeastern University and they wrote my Daddy that I had been "permanently excluded" from the College of Arts and Sciences. I said, "Don't get so upset, Pop, I can still go to Law School there 'cause they left that one out." Well Pop had a wonderful sense of humor, but that time I had a *failure to matriculate* and we had a *failure to communicate*. Too bad child abuse wasn't politically incorrect back then.

Anyway it was really an educating experience for her to get educated up there because she found out that the folks up

North were more prejudiced about the fact that she might be prejudiced than she was prejudiced. I think the deal was that they talk about having an eclectic (that means a bunch of different kinds of folks from all over) community for a student body and since she was from South Georgia and she put on the application that her father was a farmer she got accepted as the token redneck in the class.

Now if racial prejudice is bad, is geographical prejudice just as bad? It should read *thou shalt not discriminate by race, sex, creed, nationality, or because of where yo' crib is at.* The main reason I think geography should be included is because once upon a time geographical discrimination caused a terrible conflict called "~~The War of Northern Aggression~~" "*The War to End Slavery*"

Anyway, back to the birds. They tell me that geese mate for life. So if you watch the hunting shows on ESPN and you see a goose get shot, well, the mate just keeps circling and looking. I can't think of anything much sadder. Yes, I have goose hunted one time. I didn't kill one because I never have been too much threat with a shotgun, but a friend of mine did. You could hear it whistling through the air like a 747 crashing and it hit the ground with such a thud that it bounced me in the air. And you know what? The thing didn't even taste all that good to me. What's the point?

Well I don't imagine a gull would taste too good at all. I am prejudiced. I'm highly prejudiced against folks who kill gulls with their cars and if I were King of the Forgotten Coast, I would lock those folks up in stocks on the causeway and hang signs that said "THIS PERSON KILLED A GULL WITH THEIR CAR." And I would keep them locked up until the end of mating season so the gulls could fly over them and do whatever they wanted to on them.

THE EXPANSE ACROSS THE BAY

The expanse across the bay was causeway, then low bridge, then causeway, then high bridge over the Intracoastal Waterway. The feeling began as soon as I saw it. The sunsets were always the best because you were traveling to the west. I always wanted to arrive here that time of the day. I remember coming across with my mother, the artist. She has always been an artist, but she didn't always paint. She was an artist when she married my father but she gave up painting to dedicate herself to my father and us, but she is an artist at being a wife and a mother. After my father was gone she painted again, maybe better than before. I wonder how great she would have been if strokes had not made it impossible for her too frail little hand to guide her brush?

When we traverse the bay she describes the colors in the clouds, the sky and the water. I can see some but not all of them but I always see them when I see her paintings and then I know why she is an artist and I am not. Mama is many things I am not. She sees things in people better than I. A lack that continually causes me many struggles, trials and tribulations.

One day when we reached the "high hump" of the John Gorrie Bridge above the intracoastal waterway, below appeared a beautiful little fishing village with the waterfront on the starboard, tree tops with metal roofs poking through and the bay aport. We were moving to our new home, Apalachicola, Florida. A move I should have made twenty years ago because immediately wonderful things began happening in our lives. Mama loves this time of year because she has always been an avid bird watcher, especially coastal waterfowl, so she loves to see all the different gulls nesting on the St. George Island causeway. She keeps a book on what birds she has seen and when and where; and of course she loves the Purple Martins that come each spring to the house we put up for them.

There is a gull I often see when I am traveling *back and to* to the Island to work that has a gimp leg that hangs down when he flies. I call him "Peg." I saw him on the causeway the other day in the nesting area and I thought, "That tickles me to death that Ole Peg can find a mate and have a family even with a gimp leg."

Some folk's frailties are on the outside and some folks have them on the inside, and then a lot of us have them in both places. I don't think Ole Peg would ever get to be the stunt bird for Jonathan Livingston Seagull, but he seems to be able to do just about every thing else. For some crazy reason I always feel like that old bird is watching over us.

Mama and I have been kicked back and gotten up and gone again many times. The doctors have told us that Mama won't be able to get up and go again this time; the cancer has spread everywhere. You know what? She's beautiful and cheering up all around her. She's ready to go be with my Daddy.

I don't know what's ahead of us but somehow with all of our wonderful friends and Ole Peg we will get back up and go on. It's funny how I feel a real sense of serenity now. Many times I wondered what Robert Frost meant. Now somehow I think I know.

STOPPING BY WOODS ON A SNOWY EVENING
By Robert Frost

Whose woods these are, I think I know,
His house is in the Village though,
He will not see me stopping here,
To watch his woods fill up with snow.

My little horse must think it queer,
To stop without a farm house near,
Between the woods and frozen lake,
On the darkest evening of the year.

He gives his harness bells a shake,
To ask if there is some mistake,
The only other sound's the sweep,
Of easy wind and downy flake.

The woods are lovely,
Dark and deep.
But I have promises to keep,
And Miles to go before I sleep.
And Miles to go before I sleep.

Mama and the Retirement Home

I have been going through some pretty difficult times. Since I came home from fighting the Communist Insurgent Guerilla Forces in the Viper Infested Jungles of South East Asia I have not had a bad day nor a bad week, but even good times can be hard and, as anyone who lived through the Great Depression will tell you, even bad times can be good. (I heard so much about the Great Depression when I was growing up and I felt so guilty about it that I even thought I had caused it and it was all my fault until I was about 27 years old). I think they call it "Bittersweet", but I think that anything that's bitter ain't sweet. My Mama always told me that good times don't build character; till finally I told Mama I've got about all the character I can stand.

Everybody's got a Mama, and I've got one. She's been my Mama all my life. She's the first person I ever knew. I'm a Big Mama's Boy. When I was little I never wanted to be very far from my Mama. The little church She and Daddy helped established had a quilting bee for the Ladies' Bible Study and they compiled a cook book with a picture on the cover of the ladies holding the quilt they had crafted for the missionaries and on the end stood Mama, with me beside her holding her skirt and sucking my thumb. I had to get braces later on to correct my buckteeth. I even have a scar where I fell out of the bed one night on my face, and my teeth protruded so badly that they penetrated my lower lip. Heaven is sucking your thumb and holding your Mama's skirt. When I was fighting the Communist Insurgent Guerillas in the Viper Infested Jungles of Southeast Asia, I was scared and I wanted my Mama.

Mama's beautiful, and she was the captain of the swimming team at the North Avenue School for Girls in Atlanta and later on the first Miss Orlando Florida. She and Daddy loved each other. I've never seen a couple more devoted to each other. Daddy had his last major stroke in their Gulf Front home on St. George Island, and it was a great traumatic experience for Mama. She got him home on a Sunday afternoon and I went to the hospital and sent everyone home to rest and spent the night with Pop. He woke up early the next morning and he was clear as a bell, and for about the next thirty minutes we had the most wonderful conversation we've ever had. Then he went to sleep and when he woke he neither spoke nor ate the last year of his life. He was fed with a tube with Mama lovingly by his side until the end. That's the way she wanted to do it and the easiest way to do things is Mama's way (the pussy willow switch taught me that the hard way). Later that morning Mama and her sister, Aunt Mary Lib, came to the hospital (if I had been a girl I would have been named Mary Elizabeth but since I wasn't and Aunt Mary Lib never had any children I named one of my dogs Mary Elizabeth and she actually liked it). Mama was having trouble. We didn't know it at the time but she needed a pacemaker (as I said later we bought her a $25,000.00 pair of jumper cables) so she swooned and flopped in a chair and they came and took her to the emergency room. Well I was running down to the emergency room to see about Mama, and running back upstairs to check on Daddy, *back and to and to and fro* until Aunt Mary Lib stopped me about 10:30 in the morning and queried, "Gill, can you handle everything?" To which I respectfully replied, "Yes Ma'am", (I always did, because I used to say the difference between a rattlesnake and Aunt Mary Lib is the rattler gave you warning. You could be ditty-bopping along not doing what you were supposed to be doing and Aunt Mary Lib without warning would give you what she called a swift kick in the ......!) She said, "I have a beauty parlor appointment at 11:00." No matter what happened the "Jones Girls" never missed a beauty parlor appointment.

Well Pop's gone and so is Aunt Mary Lib. I had to take care of her when she got ill and that was an honor. Then when I unexpectedly wound up living alone, I let Mama come live with me because she didn't want to go to a retirement home and that was even a bigger honor. Of course she came with me when I moved to Apalach and she lived with me for two years and six months before moving to an assisted living home in Mexico Beach. The hardest thing I have ever done was to talk to Mama about going, but you know she wanted to and she is really happy. She's got lots of friends and the people there are really nice to her and I've gotten some peace of mind in the deal (that is, in what little piece of mind I have got left.) I have a Florida room in the front of our house (a glassed in porch- we also have carriage house - a garage apartment) and I sit out there every evening and folks drive by really slow and rubberneck. The other evening I said to myself I bet those people are looking at this beautiful house and my three boats and they're saying, "That's a lucky man that lives in that house." And I thought they're absolutely right, but they just don't have a clue.

It about kills me that Mama's over there but that's just Charlotte's Web. She's the last one of both sides of my family. The Depression/W.W.II generation was really something. They don't make them like that anymore, but I guess what bothers me the most is that when they are gone, we're next.

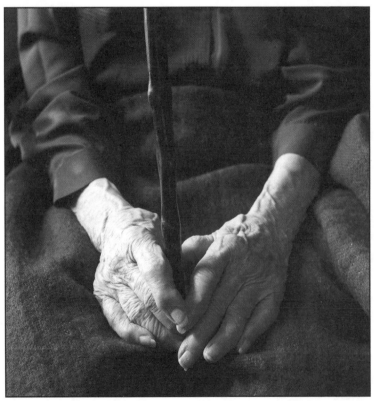

DOG YEARS

Saturday was my birthday. I didn't announce it in advance because I knew all of y'all would send me a present and I didn't want to have to write a bunch of thank you notes. I did get everything I needed but not nearly as much as I deserved.

I won't tell you how old I am but if I was a dog (and some folks think I am) I would be 378 years old. I have two dogs, Isabella Rossellini and Black-eyed Susan. If they were people (and they think they are) Isabella would be 70 and Susan would be 28. Isabella has arthritis and can't get around too well. Susan is a bird dog, a pointer; and she is really good because she will point anything - birds, lizards, rabbits, sparrows, sand crabs and yes, even quail. But what she really likes to point are bugs. I planted a bunch of butterfly bushes in my yard and we don't have a lot of butterflies but you wouldn't believe how many bumblebees we have. Well Susan spends hours staring down bumblebees and when one comes close she tries to snap it. I told her she better leave those critters alone, but like most women I know she doesn't pay too much attention to what I tell her. You guessed it! This morning I thought I heard a baby crying and went out into the back yard and Susan was laying there rubbing her snout with her paws and when I went home at noon her lip was pretty swollen. We used to go crabbing and I tried to tell a lab I had named Jenny (the Pride of Jennings Bluff who lived to the ripe old age of 112) the same thing but she wouldn't listen either until one day an ole blue crab got her by the nose. Who said crabs can't fly?

Susan is so smart she can talk. I'll tell her to sit and then I'll ask her, "Susan, what's on top of the house?" And she will say, "Woof--Woof." I just can't correct her speech impediment.

Pets are wonderful. I get in the doghouse sometimes (I usually deserve it), but no matter what I do Isabella and Susan are glad to see me, and my Mama is too. I only remember my mother being genuinely upset with me one time and that story is unpublishable.

One of my favorite pets of all time was an alley cat I adopted. He was solid black except all four feet were white so I called him Billy White Shoes Johnson. Now I had bought an old house and restored it, and it was in a not too good section of town - a tough place for a cat to live. Well Billy would stay out all night and come home some mornings all torn up and bleeding. His right front leg got so chewed one time that he lost it. So he became a three-legged cat and I told him if he didn't quit living on the wild side he might end up being called Billy White Shoe Johnson. He got along good with three legs and he could run just as fast as ever but he had a little trouble stopping as good as he wanted, and some times he would run into things. He finally died and the Vet said it was from liver failure. That's what happens when you stay out carousing all night. Since he was adopted I don't know how old Billy was. People would ask me how he lost his leg and I told them, "He kept going to the bathroom in the house so I cut his leg off." You should have seen their expressions.

As you know my Mama lives with me and her birthday was Sunday. If she were a dog she would be 602 years old and her job is to take care of Isabella and Susan. She loves them and they love her. I guess all in all I'm pretty lucky to be living with three wonderful ladies.

MAMA'S GONE

Last month I wrote that my poor little Mama was very ill; now, I regret to report that she passed away. It has really been a hard time for me but I'm doing well and thankful for the time I had with a lovely lady and thankful for all my wonderful friends. So I thought I would write about her one more time and then let her rest in peace.

Mama really was beautiful; she was the first Miss Orlando, Florida, in 1934. Of course she was a southern lady and very proper about everything. Everything had to be in order and on schedule. Here's some of my favorite Mamaisms.

"If you mind your own business, some day you will have a business of your own." I particularly like this one and I have kind of made it my motto.

Don't ever at the end of one of Mama's delicious meals say you are full as a tick. You may say either, "You have eaten sufficiently" or "you have dined sumptuously."

Now pay particular attention to this; it is very important to rotate your plates every week. You say, "What?" Yes, you see, unless you are having dinner parties regularly, the china on the bottom of the stack doesn't get used, hence it doesn't get washed.

Mama changed her sheets every Saturday morning and of course that meant I made up the bed (I had plenty of this training in the Marines; you could make a quarter bounce off Mama's bedspread, and she always had hospital corners on her sheets) because she was too frail. But once a month she had me flip her mattress so it wouldn't get a hole in it where she slept, and every other month we not only flipped it, we rotated and flipped it.

Now when Mama was traveling, she always washed out her underclothes and hung them up at night to dry because she would never put dirty undergarments in her suitcase. And of course the famous one was to "Always wear clean underwear because you might have a wreck and if you go to the hospital they might have to take your pants off." Well, I probably won't follow that rule all the time now, but at least I'll turn them inside out once a week.

Mama and Daddy loved St. George Island. We came down every year for vacation until finally they bought a beach house. The whole family came; five children and eight adults. We caught all our own fish, crabs, and shrimp and we usually only went out for dinner one or two nights during the two weeks. That meant a lot of fishing, crabbing, and shrimping. So I made my Daddy an offer he couldn't refuse. "Pop" I said, "I'll take the kids out fishing all day and burn them up and wear them out so they will go to sleep at night and not stay up and bother everybody, and you can buy gas for the boat and all the beer I can drink." He said that was the best deal he had ever heard. The next summer just before we left to come down, he asked me "Son, what would you think if I just bought you only half of the beer you can drink?"

Well the first day I didn't take the kids fishing. I claimed that something was wrong with my boat, and it wasn't long before Pop went back to the old deal.

Mama had two sisters, Aunt Mary Lib and Aunt Margaret. They were all beautiful; Aunt Mary Lib was a model in New York during her youth and if I had been a girl I would have been named Mary Elizabeth, but I wasn't and she never had any kids so I named one of my dogs Mary Elizabeth, and you know, it really tickled her. (It's going to take a whole nother newsletter to tell y'all about Aunt Mary Lib). Aunt Margaret was a great scallop shucker. We would all go get a mess of scallops and bring them back to the beach house, and Aunt Margaret and I would get under the house with some cold beer and shuck and talk for about three hours.

The biggest mess I ever got into was one day those three old ladies came to me and said, "Gill we want to go to the lighthouse on Little St. George", to which I gave my standard reply, "Yes'um." Well I got my old homemade mullet boat, the "Miss Kerniebelle", gassed her up and launched her, and I loaded up those three old ladies and we headed out. I had them sitting up on the net table in some of those sawed off beach chairs. Of course they all had on one-piece bathing suits. The "Miss Kerniebelle" was painted hunter green with an iron pipe painted red, bolted in for the shrimping pole. She was real purty. Well we got through the Cut and around to the lighthouse, and I dropped them off in the surf and they swam ashore to do some sightseeing and shelling. I pulled a little ways out and dropped my shrimp net overboard to see if I couldn't trawl up a few shrimp cocktails for supper. Now this is a true story (which when folks tell you this, that normally means it's a lie but this really happened). The first pull, I got the net up on the net table and I saw a fish that looked like a flounder but was shaped like a guitar. I had heard of it and I know about it now; it was a guitar fish. It's electric like an electric eel. Well I reached down to untie the bag and touched that dang thing and it sent a jolt all the way up to my elbow - almost knocked me off the back of the boat! That would have been really cute if I had drowned with them on the beach. It took three days for my arm to quit hurting. Now here came the problem; dumping those old ladies off in the surf was easy but picking them up was a mess. They were all on either side of seventy years old and couldn't hoist themselves into the boat so I finally had to anchor and swim between their legs and pick them up on my shoulders and dump them onto the net table. To my recollection that was the last boat trip they ever made. Pop had his last major stroke at the beach house with just him and Mama there, and it was such a traumatic experienced that unfortunately she sold it.

Oh yea! One thing Mama always wanted me to remember (she wrote it in the front of the New Testament she gave me at the airport as I was leaving to go fight the Communist Insurgent Guerilla Forces in the Viper Infested Jungles of South East Asia and I carried it in the pocket of my flight suit every day): the inscription read, "To Gill, with all our love, Mama and Daddy, January 1969, Psalm 119:105."

SHOPPING LIST

S ome folks ask me, "Why haven't you written your newsletter lately?" and I retort, "I'm sorry." And they say, "Oh, you don't have to apologize." And I reply, "I'm not apologizing, I'm just telling you my state of condition, I'm sorry, i.e. no good."

Any way, can you believe how low interest rates have gotten? They are lower than when I started in banking in 1973. I was 27 years old. I decided to make a little survey so I went in the bank today and asked one of the account executives (that's what they call them now), "What is your passbook savings rate today?" Of course that query was met with a blank stare because you don't get passbooks anymore, but I was told a money market account will yield 1.5% and up according to the balance.

When I was young my mother used an archaic method of stocking the pantry called a *shopping list* because we lived way out in the country. Here's the way it works. You keep a pad in the kitchen and every time you run out of something you write it on the list. Likewise if you think of something you need, and then once a week or less often, you go to town to the store and do your shopping for the next week or longer. I have searched all of the local and state statutes and I can find no law that requires you to go to the grocery store every day (or twice a day usually in my case). I'll bet some of the folks out towards the Cape or on Dog Island have rediscovered this ritual.

There was another peculiar habit that folks had in the olden days called *saving*. Some may find this hard to believe but I was in college before Satan invented credit cards so if you wanted to buy something you had to save up the money first and pay cash. Here's how it worked. You went to the bank and opened a passbook savings account and they gave you a little ledger book, and regularly each week or so you would go to the bank and deposit money in your passbook, and the teller would enter the amount and bring your balance current and stamp it to make it official. Then every three months you could come in and they would enter your interest because most accounts compounded quarterly instead of daily. My Daddy took me to his bank to open up my passbook savings account when I was six years old. I have that old thing somewhere and I have looked for it, but I swear I think it paid 2.5%.

Where did a six-year-old get money? You're right, I saved it from little odd jobs and from money relatives gave me for Christmas and my birthday. Later my Daddy decided that I needed to learn to budget my income (another outdated tradition as forgotten as the coast we live on) so he announced that I would receive 25 cents (you know I just noticed my computer has a dollar sign but not a cent sign; now does that tell you anything?) a week to spend any way I wanted. So every Saturday afternoon we would go to the movie to watch the latest western and, of course, the serial that had a new episode each week. The movie cost 14 cents, which left me a dime and a penny. Now I would buy a fudgecicle for 5 cents and save 6, or a coke and popcorn for a dime and save a penny, but usually I came home with 6 cents and put it in a piggy bank until I had a few dollars to take to the bank and put in my passbook savings. Later I got a job making big money but it didn't last. I was hired to bail hay for a dollar a day, but since I wasn't big enough to lift a bale by myself I wasn't of much use.

One of the things I had to do to get the 25 cents was to mow the grass every Saturday morning. Now that was no light task because our yard was three acres and it took me the better part of the morning. But it wasn't too bad because Daddy bought one of those powered mowers with rolling blades, then he bought a little tractor-like seat with two wheels and hooked it to the lawn mower, thus making one of the first riding mowers. Well it had a lot of power and it was fast and since our three acres had some pretty long straightaways, I would get it cranked up pretty good and get that job over quick. Well that went along really well until some people built a house next door (as I told you we lived out in the country and for a long time there was no one around). It wasn't the crowded neighborhood that bothered me, the people had a daughter my age and that age was 12. Well that was about to drive me crazy and the worst thing was her bedroom was on our side of the house and she had a big double window. Well early one Saturday I was mowing along at top speed and I noticed her curtain was ajar and I thought I could see her. While I was craning my neck, I ran square into a pine tree and tore Daddy's lawn mower to Hades and cut my leg pretty bad. I did get to know her better as time went by and one day we were in her back yard and she announced, " You can kiss me if you can catch me." And she took off and I did too, and I was about to catch her when she stepped in a gopher hole and broke her toe and they took her to the emergency room and I don't think I ever got to kiss her.

The big money I made came when I would finish the grass. We lived close to the country club and I would start walking down the clay road in that direction and pretty soon someone would give me a ride. I would caddy for $9.00, that's fifty cents a hole for eighteen holes. And I would shag balls for $2.00 a bag and that was better and easier money. I played sometimes and I still can play a little, but if I hadn't been so greedy and played more I would have probably won the British Open instead of Ernie Els (or at least be on the Senior Tour).

Where I really missed out: I started a rock and roll band when I was thirteen and we played for $35 a night (that's for the whole band). We broke up when we went to college but if I had kept it together I would probably be singing, "My Maserati does 185, I lost my license and now I can't drive. Life been good to me.....) All I had on my mind was making money and saving it, and if I had kept playin' golf and rock and roll no telling how big a passbook account I would have now. It took me a long time to learn that nothing is good in excess including moderation. But I tell you what; *Life's been good to me.*

GRAMMER

You know what bothers me all the time? Grammar! When I was in public life I used to make a lot of speeches, and the nice thing about that is if you make a mistake most folks don't know you did or at least there is no record of it unless somebody taped the speech and that only happened two times that I know of. Now that I'm writing, any errors I make in grammar are indelibly etched.

It really came home to me the other day when a friend of mine who actually has a PHD (it goes like this- BS, Bull Sh..., MS, More Sh..., and PHD, Piled Higher and Deeper) told me that it really irritated him when folks misuse I and me. Now that's always bothered a lot of folks and me. (Did I get it right?) What I do if I'm not sure is I use myself instead of I or me. Pretty slick don't you think? Here's how it works. " Today the Gulf of Mexico really looks pretty to (me or I?)". But see, I can make an end run by saying "Today the Gulf of Mexico really looks pretty to myself."

When I went to the University of Georgia all freshmen had to take an English exam, and if you failed you had to take remedial English the first quarter. Seventy some odd percent failed in my class. (I passed by four points) I know what you're thinking; that's Georgia not Florida. The truth is when I moved down here from Georgia the average IQ in both states went up.

I understand they don't diagram sentences in school any more. That's great because I never did learn how to do that. They had a lot of that on the test at UGA, which is the main reason I passed by only four points. A lot of people in this country don't even know what that is, like the man who came home and told his wife, "Honey, I bought a condomonium today." To which she replied, "Thank heavens, I'm getting so tired of wearing that diagram."

Here's another good one. The Ole Dangling Participle. Where is the beach at? (It's behind the at.) By the way, do I have one in the first paragraph? See, if I do you can think I put it in there on purpose to see if you would catch it. The truth is I'm not sure whether I do or not, so for that reason I'm not going to tell you where I think it's at.

But what I really hate is when folks try to make themselves seem intellectual by using fancy phrases. "The recent adjustment in interest rates was just an aberration and not a change in the trend of underlying market forces". That really means, "I don't have any idea what in the hell happened." "You've been very supportive." Why not just say, "Thank you, you've helped me a lot"? Universities are the worst. I got a letter from one that said, "We regret to inform you that you have been permanently excluded from the College of Arts and Sciences at ………." Why couldn't they just tell me they were kicking me out? I told my Daddy, "Don't get so mad, Pop, I can still go to their Law School or Medical School". My favorite one came from my daughter's college. "Dear Mr. Autrey, We regret to inform you that that we have found it necessary to augment your daughter's tuition". I can't tell you how relieved I was; I had been scared to death they were going to raise it.

One of the greatest authors of all time, Ernest Hemingway, won the Nobel Prize for literature for developing a very sparse style (some would say genre) of writing. He actually won the prize for "The Old Man and the Sea", which is only around 100 pages. He once said that there was not a single word that could be taken out of that book and still say what he wanted. By the way, he got the inspiration for that novel from Stephen Crane's short story, "The Open Boat". Crane was actually shipwrecked and almost died after several days in a lifeboat. He eventually did die at twenty-eight years old in a house of prostitution where he lived in Jacksonville, Florida, of complications from alcohol and his exposure in the lifeboat. We can't always choose the way we will go but I certainly like Stephen's way better than Ernest's.

Maybe if we work hard enough, one day we'll be listed in "Who's Whom."

CYBER SPACE

I've got a website and two e-mail addresses. Wasn't too long ago I couldn't even spell computer and now I don't even have to know how because I have "spell check."

All this e-mail stuff is pretty amazing. Folks used to correspond by mail. Handwriting a letter was a pretty personal thing and before the telephone, folks used to take considerable time to compose a letter and everything was well thought out. Then the phone came and letters were out and now we have e-mail and soon the phone will be obsolete. The problem with e-mail is you can't claim you didn't say it, whereas if a phone conversation wasn't recorded you could claim someone misrepresented what you said (in other words: they were lying, or the new lingo is to say "I misspoke," which means you were lying). Now, they say when you are angry you should count to ten before e-mailing somebody. They used to publish letters of famous people, "The Collected Letters of Ernest Hemingway." Will it now be "The Collected E-Mail of Capt. Gill?"

In college I actually took chemistry (I passed too, believe it or not) and we used the slide rule. I really liked it but I don't have one anymore. Some Chinese people gave me an abacus; I don't know how to use it but they say if you are really good it is faster than a calculator. (By the way if you have two or more you have some abaci.) Learning to use the thing is as hard as Chinese arithmetic.

My Daddy used to take me to the tobacco auctions when I was a kid. The warehouse always paid you as soon as the auction was over and Daddy would pay his farmers right then. He kept a hand crank calculator in the trunk of his car and he would figure the deal up with that old machine and write the man a check right there on the hood of the car. The tobacco auction was quite a spectacle in the old days. It was more like a carnival because the farmers only got paid once a year. The banks didn't finance things like they do today, so most merchants would carry them for most of the year so everybody got some money. Problem was, some times there wasn't enough money. I'll never forget one time, I must have been about eight years old, Daddy had bought me an RC Cola and a bag of boiled peanuts and told me to sit down on a sheet of tobacco and wait until he got back. Well I was right in front of the cashier's cage where the farmers got their checks. (There was a pretty cute girl that worked in there. She was way too old for me but I was in love with her for a long time without her ever knowing it.) Anyway this farmer got his check and was walking by me looking at his check and he looked down and saw me and said, "Son, it's times like this when I recall what it says in the Beatitudes- Blessed are they who don't look for nothin' 'cause then they ain't disheartened when they don't get nothin'."

The most amazing tool that seems to have gone by the wayside is the CPU-26A/P, that's military for the whiz wheel, a pretty cool instrument used for air navigation before the GPS, etc. I found mine the other day while cleaning out the garage. When you planned a cross-country flight with the whiz wheel and took off, they called it dead reckoning. (I never liked that term at all. Why didn't we say live reckoning? I'm like Lewis Grizzard; he wouldn't fly because you had to go to a terminal to get on a plane.) The first time I used the whiz wheel was my first cross-country in flight school. I had everything planned out and I took off in my little helicopter. It was hot and they took the doors off for ventilation. It also helped to keep the helicopter in trim because if it got out of whack you just stepped on the pedal next to the door the wind was coming in and it straightened up. So I was flying along and I got to looking at things on the ground and the next thing I saw was my map floating down to terra firma because I had gotten out of trim and it blew out the window. Well it wasn't long before I was lost and about out of gas but I found a road and started flying IFR (I follow roads). Pretty soon I came to an intersection and lo and behold I saw a building with a beautiful Pure Oil sign in front so I circled around and came to a hoover (that's when you first learn to fly and you can't hover too good) and sat down next to the pump. I walked up to the station and an ole cowboy was sitting there with his hat pulled down over his eyes and he looked up and said, "What'll it be?' And I said, "Fill'er up." I went in side and got myself an RC Cola and espied exactly what I was looking for- a Pure Oil map of the great state of Texas and I grabbed one as they were free back then. Well I paid for the gas and the ole boy sat back down and pulled his hat down over his eyes and I asked him, "Aren't you curious why I landed at your station to get gas."

And he said, "Yep, I sure am, most folks land across the street at the airport."

Hope to see y'all on the Internet.

SUSAN AND RAMSEY

The first time I saw Black Eyed Susan she was in a litter of puppies in a dog pen at a quail hunting preserve. She had a solid black tail with a white tip and she had black spots on white with a black patch over one eye, thus her name. Every time I went to the dog pens, which was every day, she was all the time looking at me waving that tail like a flag. Well I was going through a pretty bad time and I needed a friend, so one day I said to her, "Come on pup, I'll get you out of this pen and you can come live with me." So off we went.

Now, I lived right across from the pens and for the first couple of days when I let her out she would run over to the pens and get under the dog house. I would have to go and fetch her home until one day she got about half way to the pens and she looked at the pens and then back at the house and she turned around and scampered to the front porch and waited there for me until I got back. What a great friend she became too, a blessing for both of us.

Well now, Susan was special to many folks because she was afflicted, having been run over by a car that broke her back. The local vet thought the best thing to do was to put her down unless I took her down to the University Hospital in Gainesville. Maybe they could do something, so off we went, as I couldn't handle the alternative and Susan didn't think much of it either.

Well, it's a pretty good little ride down there from Apalach. I had Susan in the back of my Land Cruiser lying on a quilt my Grandmother had made by her own hand and she would have been proud for her to use it too. Susan was rasping mighty heavy the whole way and I was driving as fast as I could. I didn't even stop at the Dixie Nut House at Old Town at the Suwannee River to get a bag of boiled peanuts. Right before I got to Gainesville it came a gulley washer and I could only go about fifteen miles per hour. In a little bit I could no longer hear her breathing, so naturally I thought she was gone but when I got there she was still with us. Now this hospital is a wonderful facility, and the first specialist was a neurologist who determined that Susan still had feeling in her hind quarter. A young surgeon had developed a new technique whereby he pinned the spine through the skin without operating and held the pins in place with a metal plate. The operation was a success and I was told that it would be six to eight months before she would walk if at all. Well in about three weeks she was hobblin' around the yard with this metal contraption on her back getting hung in the bushes and scaring me half to death.

I had always thought folks were crazy to pay $5000 for a bird dog and now I had one, worth every penny too. About a year later her doctor got in touch with me and wanted us to come to Gainesville so he could film a video of Susan. He was giving the keynote address at a national veterinary conference and Susan would be the focus of his presentation.

Of course she was pretty tickled and that's the sort of thing I always admired about her. After she became a celebrity she still spoke to all her friends in Apalach and you could never tell she was famous by the way she acted.

Susan went home July 16th in the year of our Lord 2009. My little bird dog had been with me some thirteen years before she left us for the big quail woods in the sky and left a hole in our hearts and our lives. That was the third pet Lane and I had lost in less than a year, so we resolved to take a break and think things over and not rush into anything.

I've always kinda had a rapport with animals, children, and old folks. It's the ones in the middle I seem to have a problem with from time to time. One Sunday pretty soon after we lost Susan, Lane and I were headed to St. George Island to walk on the beach and throw my mullet net so maybe I could bushwhack our dinner, when for no particular reason I had this tremendous urge to go to the Humane Society. Now, I hardly ever go to one because I can't stand to walk out and leave all those pitiful little critters behind. Anyway Lane agreed to go with me, even though she didn't think enough time had elapsed. We had agreed, if we got another family member, it would be feline so we would downsize, so to speak.

Well when we got there the cat room was full and the cats were running everywhere, but this one little fellow kept rubbing up against my leg. I have never seen an uglier creature. He was kinda of a tabby yellow but really he didn't have much fur at all, sorta bald, with these weird slanted eyes, greenish with black pupils. Actually, to tell the truth, he looked like some kind of space alien. So we left and went mulleting and walking.

Now Franklin County has the most active Humane Society per capita anywhere I know about (probably the largest AA Chapter per capita too but let's don't get correlation and causation mixed up). Many local shops keep orphaned kittens in cages ready to go home with anyone, papers and all. I think last year Apalach adopted out eighty some odd kitties. At the time Lane and I were operating her photography shop in a nice little white frame building behind the Grady Market so, she being smarter than I, suggested that we keep a few kittens in our shop sorta having them out on approval. So off to Eastpoint I went to pick out three critters. After selecting what I thought were the best candidates, I asked the director to pack them up and I would be on my way. Well I went out to my car to get a space ready for the cage and when I got back, lo and behold, she had packed up that *ugly thing* instead of another one I had picked out! But I felt so sorry for the little fellow, I took him anyway.

Well, things worked out pretty well at the shop except for it being a little too small, but folks liked the kittens and said how cute they were except when they looked at the *ugly one*, they didn't say anything (if you can't say anything nice, don't say anything at all my Mama always said). But I was warming up to him because what he lacked in beauty he more than made up in spunkiness. Then Lane went away for the weekend to be with her girls and left me in charge of the shop and the kittens. Since we were closed on Sunday and Monday I decided to take them home on Saturday night and not make them stay in the cage all weekend. As soon as I let them out, two of them ran under the sofa and stayed there until I fetched them out Tuesday morning and the *ugly one* stuck to me like a sticktight, rubbing against my leg or sitting in my lap purring whenever I sat down. There was only one problem, and I learned this from a cat lover, sometimes kittens have a nervous condition in new surroundings whereby they emit offensive odors on a regular basis. He was so cute and loving I put up with it.

When Lane came home we decided the shop was too small to keep the kittens. I loaded them up and took them back to the Humane Society and left them with a guilt-ridden heart. Lane could tell it too, so she said for me to do whatever I wanted. I sure did miss that little fellow even with his obnoxious habit. After a day or two I told Lane I was going back and if he had been adopted, it would be for the best.

The director let me in the cat's quarters and, of course, they were running all over the place but my little friend was nowhere in sight. My heart sank, and I was just about to leave when I felt something rubbing against my leg. I grabbed him and told the lady I felt I had to adopt him because he was so ugly nobody else would.

He's great. The President of the Humane Society told us he is an Abyssinian, an Egyptian breed and the oldest breed of cats known. You can see them in the pyramids, so we named him Ramses II since he must be a reincarnation of the greatest pharaoh. Ramsey, as we call him, is the smartest little kitty cat in the whole wide world.

GORGEOUS GEORGE AND GRANDMAMMA'S PENNY

My Uncle Roddy and Aunt Margaret lived on Tupelo Street in Atlanta, kinda foretellin' since now I live in the land of Tupelo Honey. Their house was two bedrooms with one bath, sorta tight for them and their two daughters. It was especially tight when we, my family of four, visited, which we did often - I loved it because they were great folks. We had to drive up two-lane US 41 from Valdosta with no a/c in the car. Daddy had a ventilated seat cushion but his back was always soakin' wet and every so often he would lean forward and Mama would pull his shirt lose from his back. My sister and I had a milk bottle in the back because Daddy wouldn't stop. I always thought my sister was at a considerable disadvantage in the toiletry arrangement. The trip usually took about eight hours, compared to maybe three and a half now, with getting behind pulp wood trucks and the like goin' about forty miles an hour.

I always got on great with Uncle Roddy and as I said he had two very special daughters, but I could kinda tell he might have wanted a son too, so I guess I was the surrogate. They had a black and white TV with a rabbit-ear antenna on top, many years before we had such in Valdosta. One of

Uncle Roddy's favorite things to do was watch Live Atlanta Wrestlin' and I loved to watch it with him too. Our favorite wrestler was Gorgeous George, a hulk with beautiful blond hair all in curls from a permanent, probably a Toni Home Permanent. He would enter the ring wrapped up in a cape and go through all kinds of antics before exposing his body to the women in the audience. They would all howl when he threw his cape off. The match would go pretty normal until his opponent would muss George's hair and then he would go into a rage and usually dispatch the villain. Years later I heard an interview where James Brown gave Gorgeous George credit for inspiring his act to come out with a cape and go through all his antics.

Uncle Roddy ran his family's business, the Orange Crush bottling plant, until the general demise of that soft drink. Then he sold bottle caps to bottling plants all over the Southeast and did really well because everybody loved Uncle Roddy. I don't remember what precipitated the occasion, but I took a long road trip with him one time calling on folks. We got to talk a lot and I have always cherished that time.

My Grandmamma Jones lived to be 102 and was in excellent health up to a little while after her centennial birthday. She was really old school, graceful with perfect posture. At 89 her aorta began to split and the doctor told us that she might live six months or a year but not much chance after that. We asked him what we could do and he said it might help if she had a drink every night. Well, of course, she had never touched a drop, or smoked, or any of that stuff, so every night Daddy would fix her a different cocktail until she finally decided she liked a gin and tonic. From then on she had one every night up until just before she died with no further aorta problems. As a matter of fact we threw her a big 100th birthday party at the Country Club and the proprietor of the Wagon Wheel Liquor Store where she always traded gave her a big bottle of Beefeater's all wrapped up.

She was so remarkable that when she lost the circulation in her foot and her toes became gangrenous and they told us they would have to take her foot off, she said they would not do anything of the kind. Lo and behold it healed! The doctors were stunned, as they said that was not possible.

When I was going to school in Chattanooga we always rode the train *back and to*. Some times when we were waiting at the station we would put pennies on the track and the locomotive would run over them and they would be flat as a pancake (actually a whole lot flatter than that). Well, I gave one to Grandmamma and she was really tickled but I forgot about it as time went by.

Going up, the train left at 6p.m. and got to Chattanooga about 6a.m. so our parents would get us a Pullman sleeper. One of the guys was pretty skinny so we pulled the berth down and when he laid down on it, we shut him back up in the wall. We got the Porter and told him we couldn't get the thing down, so when it flopped open, Charlie had his eyes rolled back in his head like he was dead. We never saw that Porter again the rest of the trip.

Well, I never have understood how it could happen to a sweet little innocent boy like me, but I wound up in the United States of America Marine Corps destined to fly helicopters and fight the Communist Insurgent Guerrilla Forces in the Viper Infested Jungles of South East Asia. So the inevitable day came and all the family was gathered at the Valdosta Municipal Airport to see me off, in my Marine Officer's uniform, to God knows what, when all the sudden I couldn't find Uncle Roddy. After a short search I found him behind one of the pillars crying like a baby. I grabbed Grandmamma Jones and gave her a big hug, and she put a flattened penny in my hand and she said, "Now Gill, I mean for you to bring this penny back to me, it's mine."

Well, the old Southern Airways plane was a tail loader. I was standing by the ramp when the engines fired up and if things weren't bad enough Little Gill, about two and a half, grabbed hold of me with a death grip and had to be pried loose. As we taxied out I was waving out the window and the stewardess was an old classmate, and I said, "O Lord, please don't let this brave Marine cry." Then the floodgates opened up and she came over with such kindness and put her hand on my shoulder.

I did bring Grandmamma her penny home. I drilled a hole in it and wore it on my dog tags with a St. Christopher's medal, and kept the New Testament in the pocket of my flight suit that Mamma and Daddy had given me when I left for the Marine Corps. On the flyleaf was inscribed, "To Gill, with all our love, Mama and Daddy, January 1969, Psalm 119:105."

IN COUNTRY CHRISTMAS

I've been trying to write a newsletter but I guess I have writer's block. I started one about Christmas but I didn't like it so I quit. Then I started one about who was going to be the President but that got resolved before I finished it so I canned that one. I did have one line in it I liked, "Some folks want to grow up to be the President, now they just want the President to grow up."

Folks ask me, " Have you lived here all your life?" I say, "Not yet." Then they ask, "Did you grow up here?" and I say, "Not yet." The problem is that around Christmas I get sentimental and reflective and I'm not my usual flippant and glib self. I don't care about the presents. I always get more than I need but not nearly as much as I deserve. Having all of y'all is more than I could have ever asked for. And I hate to sound corny but since I came back from Viet Nam, every day is Christmas or at least a special gift.

Two Christmas presents really stand out in my mind. In Viet Nam we lived in a "hooch", a rectangular plywood shack with a tin roof and sand bags half way up, then screen with tin shutters for the monsoon season. Inside were two bare light bulbs, four bunks, four wall lockers, four metal chairs, and four metal desks. Actually it was pretty nice; we weren't sleeping in a muddy foxhole. Outside was a bunker that we used at night because it was a pretty good walk to the head. Of course we stopped that the after the first mortar attack and we actually had to get in it. OK here's the crew. Myself, Jerry Gilley, a true southern gentleman from Ocean Springs Mississippi, Dave Desimone from somewhere up north who is a tooth Dentist now. (My northern geography isn't too good. I did travel all the way to Canada in my business and I learned one thing, you have the gnat line that runs along Macon, Georgia. You can tell where folks are from whether they are swatting or blowing gnats. Then there is the Mason Dixon line, but I discovered what I call the Moral Decay line. It runs through Petersburg, Virginia, and when you get north of it folks start acting mighty peculiar). Anyway Dave knitted to calm his nerves, he said, and asked us not to laugh at him. Well John Hendry said it didn't bother him, and that he would like a turtleneck. I don't know where John Hendry was from. He never talked about his family. All I know is he joined the Marines as an enlisted man and then got into the Boot Strap Program where they send you to college and when you graduate you are an officer. He had a BS degree in physics from the University of Oklahoma; I've only known two people in my life that took physics and passed. So Christmas Day came in 1970 and a cease-fire was observed. I never understood why we couldn't just observe one all the time. Anyway we prepared to have our Christmas celebration in our hooch. I had some Coors beer I had smuggled in Country, some homemade canned boiled peanuts and, believe it or not, lobster bisque that a Marine from Maine had shipped in from Salt Water

Farms. Then we decided to open our presents that had been sent from home. John Hendry was sitting on his bunk in the corner looking really solemn and dejected because no one had sent him any. I was afraid that might happen, so I reached into my wall locker and pulled out a paper sack full of some things I had sent from home for him and I handed them to him and I said, "Merry Christmas, John." He looked at me and started trembling and asked, "For me? You mean these are really for me?" I said they were and he took the bag and with tears running down his cheeks he commenced to open his Christmas.

We had an old black gentleman, Raymond "Fat" Anderson, who had worked for my father and then for me. Against all caution one day he was bailing hay and the machine jammed and he tried to get the wire out without shutting down the bailer and bailed his hand but he could still do more work than a man with ten hands. Folks would ask me how he lost his hand and I might say, "We caught him stealing." Or I might say, "He got it caught in the cane grinder when we were making syrup, but you know, that year was the best crop of syrup we ever put up." (Did you hear about the Daddy, Mama and Little Baby mole burrowing along and they came upon a man boiling a pot of syrup and the Daddy mole said, "I believe I smell sorghum syrup", and the Mama mole said. "I believe I smell maple syrup", and the little baby mole said "All I can smell is molasses.") Anyway I decided to have a company Christmas party. We had a drawing for Christmas presents and I rigged the drawing so folks got certain presents. (I figured I owned the Company and I could rig the drawing if I wanted.) So I had it rigged for Fat to get a crock-pot because he hunted squirrel all the time. Well I had no idea that he either had never gotten a Christmas present or at least not for a long time. Well when I handed it to him he got the most surprised look on his face and then he started laughing and the laugh got higher and higher until he finally started crying.

I know where Fat is; he left us about a month ago in the middle of open-heart surgery, but I can't find John Hendry. What I would really like for Christmas is to know that John Hendry is well and God is blessing him.

MERRY CHRISTMAS

KNIVES

LETTER TO LANE'S BROTHER JACK

Dear Jack,

Thanks for the knife. It's a good one and I'll enjoy it.

I've always loved knives and my Daddy said every man should carry a pocket knife. I do now, a Case I bought at the now defunct Red's Hardware in Apalach. The problem is you forget about it on a trip and now-a-days they'll take it away from you at the airport.

I remember the Christmas I got my first pocket knife (a rite of passage); I must have been about nine. We lived out in the country with lots of woods behind us and behind that a cow pasture. Next door lived the Allens, Mr. and Mrs. Allen and their son and daughter. Mr. Allen built fences for a living, the old fashioned ones with creosote posts and wire as they didn't have chain link back then. They were poor, lived in a small shotgun house without running water, just a hand pump in the back yard that you had to prime. Talk about some fine tasting water; you just poured some water from the prime jar kept at the base of the pump and pumped and pretty soon this delicious cold water would flow out to quench your thirst on a sweltering South Georgia summer day. My first lesson in thinking of others was when Mrs. Allen told me it was a sin not to leave the prime jar full for the next thirsty passer by. There was no lawn, just a dirt yard that Mrs. Allen always kept swept clean. I liked Mrs. Allen a lot and spent many hours on her back porch talking to her, and her son, a very bright boy about fifteen then. He made the first crystal radio I had ever seen and ended up going to the Georgia Medical College and becoming a doctor. They had a chinaberry tree in the back yard and Mrs. Allen would cut a branch and hollow it out, plug the end and make whistles for us. Come to think of it that's probably where my interest in music began.

Anyway, Daddy had a deep well with irrigation all over the yard for Mama's azaleas. Since we had water at the back fence, the folks with the cattle asked Daddy if they could hook our water up to a trough and of course that was fine with Daddy. They rigged a big syrup kettle up with a toilet float to keep the water level up when the cows drank it down. Well I thought that was pretty neat, and I spent a lot of time playing in that strip of woods and getting a drink out of the cattle trough. So that's what I was doing that Christmas afternoon. Poking along with my new pocket knife cutting branches and whittling and the like when I noticed a rubber hose under the leaves. I thought it was just a piece of hose somebody had thrown away so naturally I cut it in two with my knife. To my surprise a stream of water spewed out all over me, so not knowing exactly what I had done I went on home. Well the next day the door bell rang and when Daddy answered, Mr. Allen was standing there.

"Hello, Mr. Allen" said Daddy. "Won't you come in?"

"No, Sir, I just wanted to come by and ask you if you were mad at me?"

"I'm not mad at you at all, why do you ask?"

"Somebody cut my water hose and I thought you might have been upset that I hooked a hose up to the cattle trough."

Well Daddy had no idea he was supplying water to the Allens as well as the cattle but of course he was happy to do so and told Mr. Allen to repair the hose as he had no idea how it got cut. Knowing that *discretion is the better part of valor* I didn't tell Daddy about it for several years, but he got a big kick out of when I finally did.

One thing I inherited from my Daddy is if he bought somebody he loved a present, he couldn't stand it until they opened it or he told them what it was. Well, when I was about to graduate from high school Daddy started going on and on about what a great graduation present he had for me. I don't know who it was worrying the most, him or me, but we both knew we would be in big trouble with Mama if Daddy told so we suffered it out.

Daddy lived in Orlando until he was about fifteen and his two big buddies in school were Bo Randall and Buddy Ebsen, yep, aka Jed Clampett. When Daddy moved to Valdosta he had a horse and couldn't take it with him so he sold it to Bo Randall for $35. He deposited it in a savings account and the bank subsequently failed in the Great Depression so he lost his horse and his $35. So who is Bo Randall? The maker of Randall Made knives, custom knives famous all over the world. Francis Gary Powers had one when he got shot and his Randall Made knife is on display in a Museum in Moscow. Guy Clark wrote a song "Randall Knife" about his Daddy and his Randall knife that'll bring tears to your eyes. Yep, Daddy had Bo Randall make me a hunting knife with my name engraved on the blade for my graduation present.

Well, the waiting list for a Randall Knife is about five years but some time later when I joined the Marines and found out I was going to Viet Nam, Daddy got Bo Randall to put me to the head of his list. He did make me a survival knife either out of old friendship or for feeling guilty about Daddy losing his horse and his $35. The knife has a $7^{1/2}$ inch blade with a serrated top and a hollow handle to store matches, water purification pills, fish hooks, etc. Fortunately I never had to use it for its intended purpose but I did find another important function. I carried it on a web belt throughout my tour. The only place where a helicopter pilot was not protected by armor plating on the CH-53 Sea Stallion was the bubble below your feet leaving the front of the body exposed. We wore a bullet proof vest but our lower torso was exposed to enemy fire so I would pull my heavy Randall Made survival knife around so it hung between my legs. Of course, in my case the $7^{1/2}$ inch blade provided more than adequate coverage.

My most unusual knife came before I went to Viet Nam. I was in Okinawa and the Marines sent me to the Philippines to the Air Force JEST school (Jungle Escape and Survival Training). All Air Force flight personnel had to go through this school before going in Country. The Philippines have real jungles with multilayered canopies and an indigenous aborigine population living in the jungle called Negritos; small people, not quite pygmies, but the men are about five feet tall and the women a little smaller. They actually wear loin cloths and carry bows and arrows. A few have been "civilized" and one was one of our instructors. I was the only Marine in the class and they love the Marine Corps because they kicked out the hated Japanese in WWII. They would hide alongside a jungle trail and when a squad of Japanese soldiers came by single file, they would lop off the head of the last guy with a homemade knife, sort of like a machete. They made them out of a jeep spring with a bone handle and they carried them in a handmade wooden sheath. The knife was about two feet long and slightly curved and shaped a little different from a machete but heavier and cuts much better. They used the knives for all sorts of things like building huts and even making a bamboo pressure cooker to cook rice in. Well when our Negrito figured out I was a Marine he stayed about two feet behind me all the time. Before I left he presented me with a smaller Negrito Knife with a $9^{1/2}$ inch blade and it is some kind of fine weapon.

Well I've still got all of these knives except I gave the Randall Made survival knife to my son, but I really like the one you sent. We caught a mess of mullet in the cast net and I used it to fillet them and it worked really great. I'll treasure it. By the way you will find enclosed a penny. Daddy was always superstitious that it was bad luck to give any body a knife so he made me give him a penny every time he gave me a knife. I gave my Negrito friend a package of c-rations.

Thanks,
Gill

SEPTEMBER 11th

My little newsletter is supposed to be apolitical and non-denominational. The primary purpose of the meager prose is to entertain and lift the spirits of my astute readers. As a fatter of mack it's way over due and my editor might have already fired me, so you may not be reading this any way. So if you aren't reading it I've in fact been fired and am out of my misery. I thought about not writing anything because that's how I feel. Then I thought about reissuing one of my older newsletters that you probably haven't read, but I've never liked being thought of as a chicken. So here it is.

After my Mama passed away, I was moving some furniture and I pulled out a drawer and an old-yellowed piece of paper fell out. It was a letter my mama had written to Reader's Digest on May 26, 1970, apparently in response to an article she had read. I had forgotten writing it, but she quoted a letter I had written home from Viet Nam: " I did what I thought was right, and I still think I did right. Flying with the Marine Corps can allow my family to walk with their heads high and make no compromises with anyone. We can either choose a mediocre life or a worthy one. But if we choose the worthy route all along the way we will have to pay for it, and as I feel now I will gladly pay the price to have the most fulfilled life possible." You see I was a college boy and from an upper middle class family so most of my friends had gotten in the reserves or whatever to avoid going overseas. I graduated from the University of Georgia in June of 1968 with a teaching assistantship in graduate school and I was married and expecting a child all of which normally meant a deferment but I was told all deferments were cancelled after the Tet Offensive of that year. (Mr. Clinton graduated form Yale University in June of 1968? Oh well, I've always been kinda slow.)

When we came home, Jimmy Carter pardoned the ones who fled to Canada. I wish he could have pardoned my brave friends that didn't make it home. I always respected the ones who had the guts to give up their country, but we shouldn't have given it back to them.

Mama also talked about the Great Depression and World War II. You see that generation knew the full value of what we have in this country and the heavy price they had to pay to give us the 50's and 60's. I grew up in the greatest time of our history - prosperity, peace and the birth of Rock and Roll. (I can't remember if it was in '70 or '71, but man would I have loved to be at Woodstock instead of Marble Mountain, Viet Nam. Talk about great sacrifices I made: I didn't even know that Broadway Joe had beaten the Colts until two weeks after the fact. Most of my generation has never experienced the horror that is out there.

During the National Observance of the Holocaust, I was in politics and I helped support the local events with all the honor and dignity our community could give. Cantor

Goodfriend from Atlanta was the featured speaker, and when he learned I would be in Washington during the National Ceremony at the Capitol, he greatly honored me with an invitation. Only a few hundred in the entire Nation were in attendance and I sat behind the U.S. Senators. The Cantor took me to meet Fred Friendly, the first American to enter the concentration camps. I had known about the Holocaust, but I didn't really know anything until then. I hadn't been so emotionally affected since Viet Nam. (Hitler attempted genocide of the Jews. He was pretty good, but we were better. We scored almost 100% against the Native Americans).

More people died on September 11th than died at Pearl Harbor, 58,000 died in Viet Nam, 50,000 died at Okinawa, and 1,500,000 died in the siege of St. Petersburg. There's no way to know how many we will lose in the coming months and years. No way to know what horror may lie in our future. After Viet Nam what bothered me most is, would our young men and women rise to the occasion again after the bad hand our government dealt us in that "Conflict"? We received a resounding YES! In the Gulf War, folk's like Colin Powell and Gen. Chuck Horner learned from our experiences in Viet Nam and vowed not to repeat our mistakes. We are in good hands. Now that our soil has been violated we know that we cannot hide our heads in the sand. People like Osama Bin Laden have always been and always will be, so now it is our mission to figure out how to protect our freedom. I don't know what the future holds but I do know one thing; the young men and women of our great country will heed the call and rise to the occasion to do what ever is asked of them. I just thank God that we have competent leadership and the support of the American people behind them.

That's the bad news. The good news is that we live in the one of the safest places in the US of A and we are surrounded by the most productive marine estuary in North America. So if everything goes to hell is a hand basket, I can get in my sailboat and go out in the bay and with my cast net. Lane and I will just have to learn to live on a subsistence diet of mullet and oysters, but then we must all be ready to make sacrifices (I have to go because Lane just told me to go out and practice throwing my net).

God bless y'all.

ROCK AND ROLL IS HERE TO STAY

One of the advantages of having an older sister is, before I was old enough to start dating, she and her friends taught me how to dance. She had an old record player that you had to put a cylinder type thing on it when you wanted to play 45 RPM records. There was this guy in town that had moved from Tennessee and he knew a dance step called the "UT". The "Shag" was really big too, having come down from Myrtle Beach, South Carolina's Miracle Strip. The "Shag" originated at a black club called Charlie's Place on the "hill" outside of Myrtle Beach. White teenagers would sneak out there, learn the dance, and then go down to the Miracle Strip and perform it. Later on I had a friend whose father owned a penny arcade on the Strip, so over time my basic dance step evolved into some sort of hybrid cross between the "UT" and the "Shag". I didn't realize it at the time but I was about to be in the middle of a musical revolution because Sam Phillips with Sun Records in Memphis was going to merge black rhythm and blues and white Rock-a-Billy to create Rock and Roll.

Before I was a teenager we would vacation with several families to Fernandina Beach, Florida. The parents would take a young black girl named Marie to take care of all us kids while the adults went out. Well sometimes she would take us down to American Beach, the only black beach I have ever known, to a juke where they had pickled pigs feet in a big jar on the counter. Marie would sit me on a bar stool and fetch out a pigs foot, put a nickel in the juke box and dance to the music while eating the pigs foot by herself, with a guy or girl whatever the case may have been. I thought it was the most wonderful thing I had ever witnessed. I loved the dancing and the music. Black music was taboo back then but a friend of mine had gone to the "Hole in the Wall" back home and heard a new singer named Little Stevie Wonder. Between the shows they put Stevie in a closet without a light but that didn't seem to bother Stevie. The nearest I came to anything as wonderful was when I was about twelve. I sneaked out and went to see Jerry Lee Lewis at the Livestock Auditorium. Mama found out about it and said, "Well, they had him at the right place, right there with the other jackasses."

My major influence came when I was twelve, my seven year old cousin came to live with us. My parents, the most considerate people I have ever known, knew I would be a teenager soon and would need my own room so they built me one over the garage. It was great. I had privacy, but there was some weird thing about the room; I could pick up the audible part of Channel 6 TV on my radio (I had a big old radio that had belonged to my grandfather, an upright thing in a wooden cabinet. It had a secret compartment in the back where I kept my switch blade, pack of cigarettes, and an unmentionable that of course I never used but all boys had to possess). That's really good exercise for your imagination.

The best thing was that I could pick up WLAC out of Nashville, Tennessee. A DJ named John R was playing soul and rhythm and blues, with sponsors like White Rose Petroleum Jelly, Silky Straight Hair Straightener, and best of all Randy's Record Room. You could order 45 RPM recordings of black artists from Randy and they would arrive in a plain brown wrapper like Playboy so folks, particularly your parents, wouldn't know you were receiving contraband through the mail. Most mornings I would wake up with the radio still playing tuned to WLAC.

Then I got shipped out. My parents wanted me to have the best education possible so they sent me off to a Presbyterian military school. Very strict, see. We were always having services of some kind. We would have these weeklong evangelistic things where, at the last service, you're supposed to come down front if you were saved. They had me so scared about going to Hell that I wasn't about to take any chances so I went down front every time. So if somebody asks me if I've been saved I tell them, "Yes, about fifty times." Anyway, every Sunday after supper we had Vespers and, afterwards it being Sunday night and everything was pretty quiet, they would only have one teacher on duty. We usually had a program, and one Sunday night we had the gospel choir from the local black high school and, of course, they gave a most stirring performance. The teacher on duty was a new English professor with a really pretty young blonde wife who was about to drive all of us crazy, so you can guess where he headed as soon as it was over. Well we were all walking out of the chapel and two of my friends who had a band turned to the choir and asked, "Hey, y'all want to go jam?" To which they gleefully retorted, "A jam! Hey y'all we're gonna jam." So we retired to a log cabin called the Senior Lodge because it was only for seniors and that's where the band kept their equipment. Well, I was a freshman, but since we were up to something unauthorized, I went in anyway and climbed up in the rafters so I could see. Soon the whole place was rocking, with boys and girls of different colors dancing with each other. I'll never forget this tall black guy with a bass voice singing Gene Chandler's "Duke of Earl". His head would bob every time he sang Duke, Duke, Duke. It was wonderful until the English teacher showed up with a face that wasn't red, it was purple.

You have to understand that this was 1960, and we had not only committed a forbidden sin, we had done it on SUNDAY !! We weren't even allowed to go to the movies on Sunday. It was a tremendous scandal, and the Headmaster was determined to find out how this thing precipitated. We all had to stay in study hall after class every day until somebody confessed. We were like Charlie in "Scent of a Woman." We held our ground, though any of us could have been expelled. Finally after two weeks the Headmaster gave up. There was no way we could have imagined the terrible things about to start happening in our country. But one thing we all knew for sure, Rock and Roll was here to stay !!!

THE RED BELLY LOUNGE AND THE GREAT MULLET SMOKER OF THE MOUTH OF THE SUWANNEE

Well it was like this right here. I was sittin' at the Bank one day mindin' my own business (my Mama always told me "Gill, if you mind your own business one day you'll have a business of your own") when in came my good customer, Delma Moss, (of Moss' Trim Shop fame. Ralf did the upholterin' and Delma ran the business end and fixed lunch every day on a little stove in the corner of their shop.) Anyway, Delma allowed that they had bought a place in Panacea and wanted to sell their place at the Mouth of the Suwannee. Well, the price seemed reasonable to me and she wanted to finance it so I got three other folks together and I became the proud owner of a ¼ undivided interest in a 1972 El Cona mobile home and lot at Suwannee, Florida.

It was a fine place, too, right on a canal with a boathouse and a 21ft. aluminum boat with a cuddy cabin. We thought that was a deal until the first time we took it out it almost sunk because some rivets were missin' in the hull.

Now Delma always was well-dressed and well-kept. She had a dressing room with a red heart-shaped divan in front of a heart-shaped mirror, which we also inherited with our furnished mobile home. They didn't leave us a TV though. But I had a black and white that the sound didn't work and Kenny had a black and white that the picture didn't work, so we put one on top of the other and we were in business, except when we had too much Old Milwaukee Lite and got the stations out of sync, then we couldn't tell what the hell was goin' on.

We were pretty happy with everything but it lacked one thing every fish camp needs, a cook shack. Well, Kenny and I planned it out, as the two other folks turned out to be silent partners. We gathered up the materials and my job was to take them to Suwanee. Kenny got a trailer and I got it loaded but it was so heavy that it fishtailed over 35mph. You couldn't keep it out of the ditch so we charted a back road, mostly dirt, route from Valdosta to Suwannee. I had the bright idea to take Little Gill and several of his friends with me and we set out. What was usually about a $2^{1/2}$ hour trip turned into a six hour trip and those boys got rambunctious and just about drove me crazy before I could get them and the materials unloaded.

Kenny wanted to build the lounge (ie. cookshack) on top of the boat house. Half of it was on the neighbor's property as the line went right down the middle and there was room for two boats, but that was good because it meant that our neighbor would pay for half of the project. We would have a pretty big place and of course Kenny and I were donatin' our labor. Now, when I say "we" built the thing I'm using the royal plural. Kenny was in the Seabees in Viet Nam (in fact the cook shack looked strangely exactly like the hootch I lived in Marble Mountain, Viet Nam, that had been built by the Seabees and most likely by Kenny himself). He could build just about anything and fast too because he was used to being shot at while he was on a project; but I was good at holdin' things in place and handin' things to Kenny.

Naturally the project turned out to take twice the time we had projected, so we finally decided to go down there and not come back until it was finished. And we did. I think we were there about four days working from the time we could see good until dark. Since it was just us, I didn't worry too much about my personal hygiene, so I didn't bother to shower too much. Now I always wondered how the Indians managed to live down there with all the mosquitoes and sand gnats, but let me tell you, if you don't bathe for several days those things won't come near you, of course neither will anything or anybody else.

Now we framed it up with only two mishaps, Kenny dropped an 8x8 beam on my head, and knocked me in the canal with his chainsaw in my hand, but we had had so many Old Milwaukee Lites by that time of the day it didn't even hurt. We dried the chainsaw out really good and it fired right up. We had planned to have cypress lap sidin' half way up with the rest screen and a tin roof with exposed beams and a wet bar and two gnat busters in the ceiling. We weren't real sure how to put on the siding so we did our neighbor's side first and learned how. His side wasn't as straight as ours but we told him it had more character and fit in better with the motif of the Suwannee than ours and that seemed to make him happy.

Now I have always been a little slight of frame so Kenny decided that I would do all the high altitude construction. I got an education on installing a five v crimp roof and installing screen. It was all finished except for the canal front, as we couldn't put a ladder in the canal. So our neighbor had a 24 ft. Pro Line and we soon figured we could tie the boat off really good and put the ladder in the boat and so we did. I ascended and commenced to install the screen. Well it seems that we tied it off side by side but not fore and aft so about the time I got started good, the boat began to back out of the slip, and all I had was about a two inch ledge to hold onto. Now it was February and pretty cold and I held on with my little fingers as long as I could until finally I had to let go and drop into the boat. Fortunately I missed the console and landed on the deck and neither the boat nor I suffered injury.

The project was finished but for a sign. We got a friend of ours who had worked his way through college painting for a sign painter, and he painted a beautiful rendering of a Red Belly with the words under it, "Red Belly Lounge" and we were mighty proud of our accomplishment. Now the neighbor I spoke of happened to be an attorney. He had a case that required a female mannequin as a prop, so after he won his case, he put her in the lounge au naturiel with her arm up waving to passing boaters. It was mighty good entertainment to sit and watch their faces when they noticed her.

You may know that guys love a project and a fish camp is not supposed to ever be "finished", so what we really needed was a mullet smoker. For years I had one planned in the back of my mind but had no impetus to actually start until Little Gill came home from school one day and said that he had a project to make something you could cook with. So I immediately said, "We're gonna build a mullet smoker" and we did and it was a nice one too. It was about six feet tall with cypress lap sidin' to match the "Red Belly Lounge"and a pitched roof which I had learned how to build from working with Kenny. It's always the hardest part. I went out to see my friend Ben Futch of "Super Cooker" fame and he built me some custom wire drawers, a metal circular fire pit, and a smoke stack with a baffle in it. And it was a beauty too and looked actually kinda like a small outhouse. But of course Little Gill and I ran way past the due date for his school project, so I think he ended up making solar tea.

Of course all folks associated with the Suwannee anxiously anticipated the maiden smoking so we planned a big week end. Little Gill and our friend Marvin loaded the contraption in my pick up truck and it took all three of us because it wasn't light. We headed out with an ice box full of chicken and sausage, but we had arranged to get the mullet when we got down there because Vernon Chewning was going to catch a mess for us fresh that day.

Little Gill asked if he could take the boat and go brim fishin' while Marvin and I cooked. That was fine, as that's why you want a fish camp so younguns can grow up doing such things. Besides Little Gill always was good help on any project. He even Kool Sealed the trailer for Kenny and me when he was only about nine years. The only problem was he managed to cool seal his new shoes at the same time so we weren't too popular for a day or two after we got home.

Anyway Marvin and I got the smoker fired up and loaded with chicken, sausage and mullet and I think we decided to have an Old Milwaukee Lite while we cooked. We decided that the thing wasn't smokin' good enough so we stoked it up and opened the baffle a little wider. Then I don't remember exactly, but I think we decided to have another Old Milwaukee Lite ("What's a home without a mother and what's a drink without another?") Before long we figured out that the problem was it wasn't getting any draft because it was sittin' flat on the ground. So we located some bricks and raised it so the air would flow properly and I think we opened the baffle a little more and man was it smokin' now. I don't remember exactly but I think we decided to have another Old Milwaukee Lite.

Well, Marvin and I were so proud of ourselves that we decided to walk out on the dock and contemplate the water and how happy all our friends were going to be with their delicious dinner. Now Marvin has a voice that's stuck somewhere between adolescence and puberty and it also squeaked a little, and pretty soon he squeaked, "I think I hear a train." And sure enough I heard a powerful roar myself but I said," Marvin, there ain't a train within a hundred and fifty miles of here." We turned around and there was a flame about six feet long coming out of the smoke stack. I grabbed the hose and Marvin ran to cut the spigot on, but the water pressure is so bad at the Suwannee that the weak stream arched and fell about two feet short of mine and Little Gill's beautiful smoker.

Well, Little Gill has always been of a calm demeanor so he didn't seem to be too surprised when he got back from fishing and saw the remnants. However, all did agree that was some of the finest chicken, sausage and mullet they had ever eaten.

HAVE FUN !!!!

Y'all had any fun lately? I have and I did it on purpose. I set out to have fun and I'm almost always successful. I was thinking today how much I like all my friends and how much fun I have with all y'all. I've told you before how being serious bores me really quick. The most miserable I have ever been was when I got out of the Marine Corps and went to work for a bank. As you know, Marines are known for not behaving all the time. For five years I had a pretty wild ride so I had a talk with myself and said, "Now Gill, you are going to be a banker and you have to be the pillar of the community so you are going to buy some nice suits and behave yourself." I made it two weeks; it was awful, but you know what I figured out is most folks don't want me to behave. It's sort of like back in 1995 when I had a little problem with my ticker. It scared me and so I quit drinking for six months, and I got along fine but the thought occurred to me, why would I give up the only thing I had ever been really good at?

Now if you go to New Orleans and stop by Pat O'Brien's, you will note that their motto is "Have Fun." It's on the glasses and match books and everything. The only purpose of that fine establishment is to "Have Fun." When I was a young banker I used to go once a year to the Young Bankers Convention and there was a group of us that were always still up having fun after all the serious folks had gone to bed. So we decided to take a trip together once a year and we went to my 1972 single-wide Elcona mobile palace on a canal at the Mouth of the Suwannee. There were five of us so we started calling ourselves the "Suwannee Five." The sole purpose of the organization was to "Have Fun" and the only rule we had was no formal business allowed. We had so much fun that a lot of other folks wanted to go on the trips with us. One trip had about 25 folks and they wanted to become members of the "Suwannee Five". We explained that if we added more members we wouldn't be the "Suwannee Five", then one of the more intelligent candidates pointed out that the "Dave Clark Five" actually had 12 members. Then we were stuck, so finally we created a new category and made them all non-voting social affiliates, which wasn't too bad since we never voted on anything anyway.

Hope to see you soon when Lane and I are out somewhere Having Fun.

THE FIRST LAST GREAT ARMADILLO RACE

I don't remember when armadillos first started showing up in South Georgia, but I was a grown man and back home from the service. I heard they crawled all the way from Texas; global crawling I reckon. I think it was about the time the coyote showed, and I guess he came from Texas too. I wondered what happened to make them want to leave.

I used to read all the local newspapers when I worked at the bank to learn of any news of my customers (one old country lawyer from Statenville referred to himself as one of the bank's victims, which hurt my feelings because that was back when banks could still be good to folks). Well, my favorite was the Clinch County News published weekly by a country scholar named Huxley. One week my issue came with a photograph of the local game warden holding up a varmint shot by a local hunter and properly identified by the game warden as a coyote. Well that caused quite a stir because we had all heard they were headed our way but nobody had laid eyes on one yet.

Next week there was a letter to the editor from a local gentleman who had purchased a dingo dog from Australia for $1500 and he identified the animal the game warden had been holding as his prized pet.

Well we were trying to promote downtown Valdosta, because a new mall had opened and the old area was no longer the center of it all. So the local merchants decided to hold a "Downtown Valdosta Day" with various events scheduled to bring the folks back to their heritage.

It so happened one morning the usual suspects were gathered at Kings Grill eating breakfast, drinking coffee and as one lady told me, "Trying to prove who was the smartest and who was the cutest." The owner and proprietor, D. J. Devane, and the infamous back woods humorist from Statenville, Willie Fred Roberts, hatched the plan to have an armadillo race. Well the plan met with unanimous enthusiasm, and folks began catching armadillos and feeding them in cages in preparation for the big day.

Now I thought it might be an endeavor in which Little Gill would like to participate. The nine-year-old boy was beside himself, but we only had one problem: we had no armadillo and lived in downtown Valdosta. Willie Fred and his crew had caught about every varmint in Echols County. So Little Gill and I called an old gentleman friend of ours, Mr. John R. Williams, who lived at Bakers Mill, Florida, inside the remnants of an old Turpentine still. Of course Mr. John R. was tickled to death to accommodate us and noted that he saw them often.

The event was scheduled for a Saturday in the spring of the year. As the day approached we had no word from John R. until he called the day before to sadly report that he had not laid eyes on a single armadillo since we called. When I told Gill he accepted the news like the gentleman he is, but I could see disappointment in his face.

Well, lo and behold the phone rang about ten o'clock that night, and it was good ole John R. telling me his dog was barking and he went outside to find he had an armadillo cornered. He had him in a trap so I said I would be in Baker's Mill early the next morning and I did leave at 6 AM and returned in time for the big race.

Well, we had been down to Joe Sing's station and gotten a Sing Bros. sticker and an STP sticker, so we decorated up our armadillo and named him "Clarence: The Central Avenue Cruiser", since we inhabited that address and downtown we went with Clarence in a galvanized trash can.

And packed it was; looked like "Downtown Valdosta Day" was going to be a big success. I remember the big race was set for 10:00 with several heats scheduled to pare the field down to the two fastest for the championship event.

Now, here's how an armadillo race works: a big circle is drawn in the middle of the street and two contestants hold their armadillo in the middle of the circle. When the whistle blows the racers are let go and the first one out of the circle wins so the critters can run in any direction. Gill's job, being the jockey, was to turn loose of Clarence, and me, being say the trainer, my job was to run Clarence down and catch him not knowing which way he would go. Well, every time Little Gill let go of Clarence's tail, he high tailed it on an azimuth headed directly towards Bakers Mill. Now all the other contestants had been in a cage for several days and even weeks being fed and getting used to being around people. They were about half tamed, where as Clarence was wild as a buck and about half scared to death. Making the championship was a breeze for Clarence, but it turned out to be torture for Little Gill, because Clarence's opponent's owner was pretty little girl named Pat, the daughter of the very organizer D. J. Devane, and the Judge was none other than Willie Fred Roberts. Gill had bragged so much about the deal, how could he face his friends if he lost to a Girl?

In spite of a bad case of nerves he composed himself enough to continue the competition, and when the whistle went off Gill turned loose and Clarence jumped straight in the air like he was shot and when he landed he took off right out of the circle while the little girl's pet just ran *back and to* like it was confused. Gill and Clarence were the champions, for sure, but my problems had just started. The crowd had gotten so big that I was cut off by a bunch of little kids before I could get to Clarence and he took off through the crowd with me in hasty pursuit. I almost grabbed him when he jumped the curb and headed into Patterson-Jones shoe store. Women were screaming and standing on chairs in their stocking feet and it was general chaos until I finally corralled Clarence in the storeroom. I came out better than in most cases, because Christie Patterson only let Clarence charge two pairs of shoes to me.

Well the grand prize was a trophy and an actual stuffed armadillo. Little Gill was tickled pink and on the way home he looked up at me and beamed and allowed as how this was the best day of his life since he had learned to water ski.

Our deal with Clarence was if he lost we would eat him and if he won we would let him go. We took him out to the Valdosta Country Club and let him go on the golf course because folks around Bakers Mill were subject to shoot the critters and some said some folks actually did eat them. Well for several years we would get reports of Clarence sightings from local golfers. The stories stopped in time so Ole Clarence either passed away or his racing stickers wore off.

So, Little Gill and Clarence retired as the all time Armadillo Race Champions because the next year some local animal rights activists at the college got their panties in a wad and the race was cancelled permanently even under the protest of D. J. Devane and Willie Fred Roberts and all the patrons of Kings Grill.

POACHED SHEEPSHEAD RECIPIE

As told to me by his honor, Ben Futch, Mayor of Lake Park, Georgia

Catch some big Sheepshead at the Pin Hook in the Apalach River. Watch your fingers and toes, as they have choppers like a human being. Carry them to Wallace at the fish-cleaning shed at Bay City Lodge and give him 75 cents apiece to filet 'em. Take 'em home and cut 'em in strips.

    1. Get your Grandma's old iron skillet out and add good salty water and bring to a boil.
    2. Drop filets in and boil until they turn white 1-2 minutes.
    3. Take out and dip in garlic butter.
    4. Eat immediately and you'll swear it's lobster and please don't "Slap yo' Mama" no matter how bad you want to.

ABOUT THE AUTREYS

Capt. Gill is a licensened USCG Captain, operating Capt. Gill's River Cruises on the Apalachicola River. Gill flew CH-53 Sikorsky helicopters in the Marine Corps, served a tour in Viet Nam attaining the rank of Captain. A former Mayor of Valdosta, Georgia, his careers include banking, securities, and tomato farming. "Lily" is his eighteenth boat as he has spent a lifetime on the water. Number nineteen has been spotted, but don't tell Lane.

Lane's love affair with photography began as a child when she discovered her Mother's Brownie camera. Throughout her career in the art - from portraiture to commercial, aerial to fine art - her greatest joy came while shooting in the early morning or late afternoon searching for the "perfect" light or what she calls the "sweet" light.

The search continues……..